MERRILL READING PROGRAM

GET SET

FIFTH EDITION

Based on the philosophy of Charles C. Fries

Authors

Phyllis Bertin
Educational Coordinator
Windward School
White Plains, New York

Dr. Cecil D. Mercer
Professor of Education
University of Florida
Gainesville, Florida

Eileen Perlman
Learning Disabilities Specialist
White Plains Public Schools
White Plains, New York

Mildred K. Rudolph

Rosemary G. Wilson

SRA McGraw-Hill

Columbus, Ohio

A Division of The McGraw-Hill Companies

TABLE OF CONTENTS

SRA/McGraw-Hill

A Division of The McGraw·Hill Companies

Send all inquiries to:
SRA/McGraw-Hill
4400 Easton Commons
Columbus, OH 43219

ISBN 0-02-674709-X

Printed in the United States of America.

8 9 10 11 12 13 14 15 RRC 09 08 07

shop

shot

ship

shut

shed

shell

shack

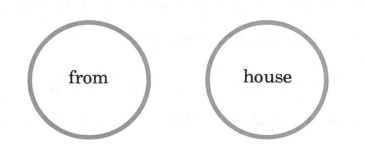

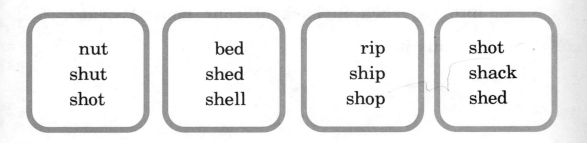

A Nap in the Shed

Dan and Jan had fun at Grandma and Grandpa's. So did Nat. He hid in the shack in back of Grandma and Grandpa's house.

Dan said to Jan, "I can't see Nat. I looked in the woods. I looked on the path, but I can't see him."

Jan said, "I bet he is in that shed in back of the house. If he gets shut in that shed, he can't get back into the house."

Jan and Dan went to look in the woodshed, but it was locked. "Grandma can let us in," said Dan as he ran to get her.

"Grandma!" Dan yelled. "Can you let us into the shed in back of your house? Nat is shut in it."

"Yes," said Grandma. "Let's go."

Dan and Grandma went back to the shed, and Grandma let them in. Nat was on a mat, shut up in the shed. He ran from the shed.

Jan said, "I bet he went in for a nap and got shut in."

"Yes," said Grandma. "Let's go back in the house. It's hot in this shed!"

The Good Little Shop

The shop was filled with

Bits of this and

Bits of that,

Lots and lots to look at,

A little ship in a jug,

A little hat, a little mug,

Figs in a can,

A pot and a pan.

Cup hooks!

Cookbooks!

A box with a shell

And a big red bell,

Cups for tots

And lots of cots!

So much to pick from

In that good little shop!

At the Shop

Grandpa had to go to a shop to look for books. "It's a good shop with lots to see," said Grandpa to Jan and Dan. "Will you go with me?"

Jan and Dan had to shop for Mom and Dad.

"Look at the ships in the jugs," said Jan. "I will get this ship for Mom."

Dan looked at a box with shells on its lid for Dad. "Your dad will be happy with this little box," Grandpa said.

"But it is so little," said Dan. "I will get that big box with the shells."

But the lid on the big box did not shut, so Dan set it back. "So much to look at and pick from," he said.

Dan and Jan looked at this and that. Dan ran six little vans. Jan went to look at a little wood box. "It has rocks in it," said Jan. Then Dan shot by Jan to look at the pets in the shop.

Dan looked at chicks in a little box. He looked at dogs and cats. "I miss Rags," he said. But he was happy to see lots of dogs and cats in the shop.

Dan ran up to Jan. "Ships, shells, dogs, cats, chicks! So much to look at!" he said.

"Yes," said Jan. "It was a bit of luck to see a ship in a jug for Mom."

Then Jan and Dan ran to Grandpa. "It's a good shop," said Grandpa. "I got six books. Did you get that ship in a jug for your mom, Jan?"

"Not yet," said Jan.

"If we can fix the latch, I will get that box with the shells for Dad," said Dan.

"We can fix it," said Grandpa. "Run and get it."

So Jan got the ship for Mom, and Dan got the big box for Dad.

"Ships! Shells! Books! Such a good little shop!" said Dan and Jan and Grandpa.

Look and Do

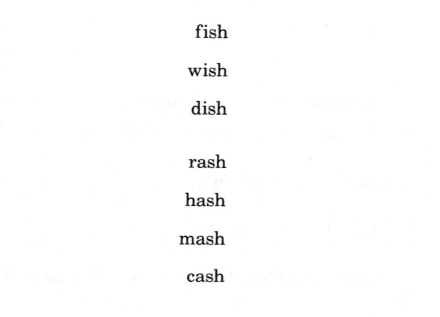

fish

wish

dish

rash

hash

mash

cash

don't   Mr.   trip

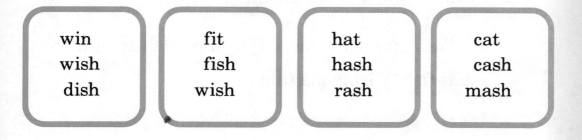

win	fit	hat	cat
wish	fish	hash	cash
dish	wish	rash	mash

13

Fish for Lunch

"Let's go catch a fish for lunch," said Grandma. "I can catch lots of fish."

"So can I," said Jan.

"Can I go?" said Dan.

"Yes," said Grandma and Jan. "Let's go."

"If we catch lots of fish, we don't have to have hash for lunch. So wish for lots of fish!" said Grandma.

Grandma and Dan got six fish, but Jan did not catch a fish.

Back at the house, Grandma cooked the fish. Jan got six yams. "Can we mash the yams?" she said to Grandma.

"Yes, mashed yams will be a good dish with that fish!" Grandma said.

A Bag To Pack

Gus and Pam have to pass Grandma and Grandpa's in Gus's van. As Gus got in his van, Mr. Bell, Dan and Jan's dad, went up to him. Mr. Bell said, "Tell Dan and Jan we miss them." Then he said good-by to Gus and Pam.

As the van got to Grandma's house, Dan and Jan ran to see Gus and Pam. Pam said, "Your dad said to tell you that he and your mom miss you. Can you go back to your house with us?"

"I don't have my bag packed," said Jan. "I will have to tell Grandma and Grandpa that Mom and Dad miss us." She ran to get them.

Grandpa was sad, but he kissed Jan. Then he said, "Go pack your bag, but I wish you did not have to go."

Grandma said, "I bet you miss Jim, Kim, and Rags. You can go back on the van with Gus and Pam. Then the cash we had for the bus trip can be yours.

"I will tell them," Jan said. She ran to tell Dan, Pam, and Gus.

"We can go back with Gus and Pam," she said to Dan. "Let's pack the bags."

"Good," said Dan. "I will get Nat so he can go with us. It was fun to be with Grandma and Grandpa, but I missed Mom and Dad."

On the Van

Jan ran up to the van with the bags. Dan said, "I can't see Nat. He has to be in that shed in the back."

Grandpa went and got Nat, and Grandma set Dan and Jan's bags on the van. "Don't forget this can, Dan," said Grandma. "That rash on your leg will itch if you don't have this."

"Do you have the cash?" said Grandpa.

"Yes, I do," said Jan. "I will miss you."

"And we will miss you, but you have to get back," said Grandpa. "Have a good trip!"

Gus and Pam said good-by. Then Dan and Jan got on the van. "Good-by, Grandma! Good-by, Grandpa!" Dan and Jan yelled.

A Fish in a Dish

	A	B

1	A fish in a dish
	    had a wish.
		A fish in a dish
		    had a wish.

2	Said the fish
	    in the dish,
		Said the fish
		    in the dish,

3	"I wish to be this,	"I wish to be this,
4	A fish in a dish	A fish in a dish
5	With a wig.	With a wig?"
6	With a wig!"	

rang

hang

sang

bang

long

song

boy   they   who

| hat
hang
rang | bat
bang
sang | song
sang
rang | lot
long
song |

Fun on the Van

Gus said, "We can have lots of fun on the van. Who will hum a song?"

"I will," said Jan. She did not hum for long.

From the van Dan, Pam, and Jan looked at pigs and horses. Then they sang a song that tells of pigs and horses.

Then Gus said, "I will tell you a story." Gus's story was of a boy who took a long trip on a ship.

"That was a good story," said Jan. Then they looked at the hills as the van went by. They looked at sheds and shacks, big hills and little hills. They looked at a big horse with a bell on its neck.

Then the van hit a bad spot. Bang! Bang! Bang! "Hang on!" yelled Gus as the van ran into a ditch.

Nat fell in Dan's lap. He did not sit in Dan's lap very long. He ran to the back of the van.

Gus went to check the van. "I can fix this," he said. As Gus fixed the van, Dan, Jan, and Pam sang songs.

"That was not long," said Jan.

"No," said Gus. "I will hang this rag on a peg in the van. Then we can go."

Then they got to Dan and Jan's house. Dan and Jan ran to see Mom and Dad.

"We had lots of fun at Grandma and Grandpa's," they said. "But we are happy to be back."

Back at the House

Dad said, "We missed you! I am so happy you are back."

"And we missed you," said Dan.

"Can we go to see Jim and Kim?" said Jan.

"Yes," said Dad, "but get your bags from the van. Then tell Gus and Pam good-by."

Dan and Jan ran to tell Gus and Pam good-by. Then they went to Jim and Kim's. They rang the bell. "Who is it?" said Jim.

"It's Dan. Can you and Kim go to my house?" said Dan.

"I will see," said Jim. He ran to his dad and said, "Dan and Jan are back. Can Kim and I go to see them?"

"Yes," said Jim's dad, Mr. Benton.

As they ran back to Dan and Jan's house, Jim said, "Kim and I missed you. I am happy that you are back. Did you have fun?"

"Yes, lots of fun," said Jan. "We went to a little shop with Grandpa."

"And we got to catch fish for lunch. Grandma has lots of songs, so we sang a lot," said Dan.

"Nat got shut in a woodshed at the back of the house. That was not fun for him, but Grandma got him and let him back into the house," he went on.

"I got Mom a little ship in a big jug," said Jan.

"And I got Dad a big box with lots of shells on its lid," said Dan.

"We went into a ditch in Gus's van. The van did not run, so he had to fix it. That was not fun for Gus. But Pam, Dan, and I sang songs and had fun," said Jan. "It was a good trip."

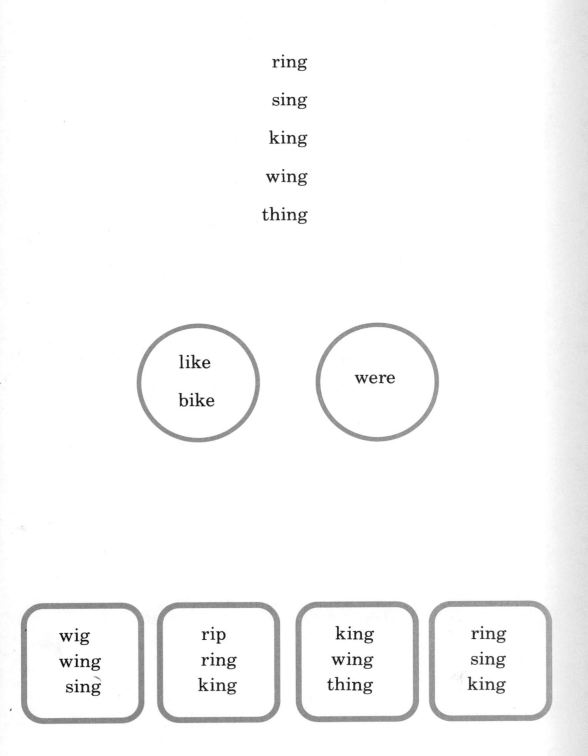

ring

sing

king

wing

thing

like
bike

were

wig
wing
sing

rip
ring
king

king
wing
thing

ring
sing
king

Back With Jim and Kim

Dan and Jan were happy to be back. Tam ran up. "I'm so happy to have you back," she said. "Did you have fun?"

"Yes," said Jan, "but I'm happy to be back."

Then Tam said, "Look at the ring my mom got me. Do you like it?"

"I like it very much," said Dan. "We looked at lots of rings and things at a little shop. But they were not like yours."

Then Jan said, "Run and get your bike, Tam."

Tam went to get her bike. Then Tam, Jan, Dan, Jim, and Kim ran the bikes on the path and into the woods. The woods had lots of things for them to look at as they went by on the bikes.

"This is fun," said Kim. "I like to go into the woods on my bike. Let's sing as we go."

"Yes," said Jim, "I have a good song for us to sing."

So Jim sang the song. It tells of a king's little boy. Then Kim, Tam, Jan, and Dan sang along.

Then Dan said, "Jan, we have to get back to the house. Don't forget Dad fixed chicken. We get to have the wings."

Tam said, "I have to get back for lunch."

"We will go back with you," said Jim and Kim. So back they went on the bike path to Dan and Jan's house.

Back for Lunch

"Are Dan and Jan back yet?" said Dot.

"Not yet," said Tom. "They went on the bike path into the woods with Tam, Jim, and Kim. But they will be back for lunch. I will cook lots of chicken wings."

Then Dan and Jan ran in. "Can Kim, Jim, and Tam have lunch with us?" said Jan.

"If they like chicken, they can," said Dad.

"Don't go," said Dan. "Will you have lunch with us? Dad cooks chicken wings. Dad's chicken wings are good! They are fit for a king!"

Then they had chicken for lunch.

"That wing was good," said Mom. "I'm happy you cooked chicken."

"Yes," said Tam. "I like your chicken a lot. It's a good thing you had lots."

"Can we go back on the bike path?" said Jan.

"Yes," said Mom. "Have fun!"

"We will," said Dan. "That was a good lunch, Dad."

Then Dan, Jan, Jim, Kim, and Tam took the bikes back on the path into the woods.

I Can Fix It

A   I can fix it.   Yes, I can.

I can fix it.

I bet I can.

B   Can you fix a pot?

Can you fix a pan?

Can you fix a box?

Can you fix a van?

A   I can fix a pot.

I can fix a pan.

I can fix a box.

But I can't fix a van.

B   I can fix it.   Yes, I can.

I can fix it,

I bet I can.

hung

rung

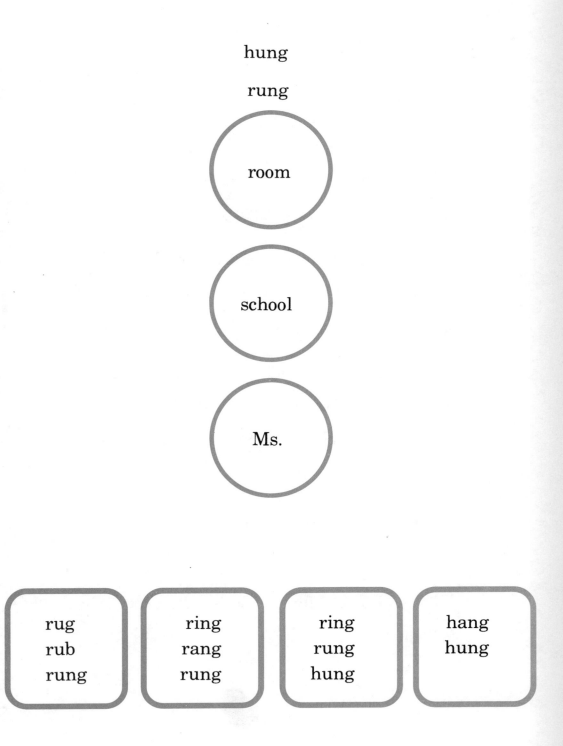

room

school

Ms.

rug	ring	ring	hang
rub	rang	rung	hung
rung	rung	hung	

Things for Tam

"Aren't you up yet?" Tam's mom said as she went into Tam's room.

"Don't forget you have to get things for school at the shop," she said.

"I did forget," said Tam. "But I don't have to get much. I will have to get a tablet and a pen. Is Dad up yet? He can go with me."

"He's up. He said he will go to the shop with you," said Mom. "I don't have much cash. Will a check do for your things at that shop?"

"Yes," said Tam, "they took a check for my jacket and cap."

"Good," said Mom. "Let's check on a check for you!"

Let's Go to School

"Let's go!" yelled Jan to Dan.

"Has the school bell rung yet?" said Dan.

"No, but we have to go to Jim and Kim's house to get them," said Jan.

"Let's see," said Dan. "I have my lunch, my tablet, my pen. Do you have your things, Jan?"

"Yes," said Jan. "Let's go!"

"Good-by!" they yelled to Mom and Dad as they ran from the house.

Jim and Kim ran from the house as Dan and Jan ran by. "I'm happy to go back to school," said Jim.

"Not me," said Kim. "I have to be in Mr. Mills's room. Is he fun?"

"Yes, he is," said Jan. "Mr. Mills lets you sing, and he will tell a story if you like. He can be fun. I am happy to be in his room."

"You, Jim, and Kim are in Mr. Mills's room. I will be in Ms. King's room," said Dan. "I wish I were in Mr. Mills's with you."

"You will like Ms. King," said Jan. "She can be lots of fun. She has a set of bells. She can tap songs on the bells. That's fun."

Pam ran up to them. "Has the school bell rung yet?"

"Not yet," said Dan. "Are you in Ms. Cook's room?"

"Yes," said Pam. "I like her. Her room will be lots of fun."

"I didn't see Tam. Is she in Mr. Mills's room?" said Kim.

"No," Pam said, "she will be in Ms. King's room with you, Dan."

By then, the school bell had rung. Pam went into Ms. Cook's room and hung up her jacket. Jim, Kim, and Jan went into Mr. Mills's room. Tam ran into Ms. King's room with Dan.

Back to School

Get your tablet! Get your pen!

School books you will get at ten.

Your lunch is in a sack.

Your pack is on your __??__ .

The kids begin to sing.

"Let the school bell __??__ ."

School can begin

If the kids are in.

The jackets are hung,

The school bell has __??__ .

We are in.

Let school __??__ !

ripped

mopped

begged

rubbed

when

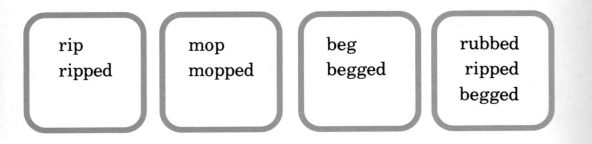

rip	mop	beg	rubbed
ripped	mopped	begged	ripped
			begged

Rags at School

When Dan and Jan were in school, Rags missed them. She looked in the kitchen for them. She looked in the bedrooms and in the bathroom. Then Rags went to school to look for Jan and Dan. She ran into Ms. Cook's room. Jan and Dan were not in that room, but Pam was.

"Ms. Cook!" yelled Pam. "That's Jan and Dan's dog! That's Rags!"

Ms. Cook said, "Jan is in Mr. Mills's room. Will you get her?"

"Yes," said Pam. She went to Mr. Mills's room. "Mr. Mills, Jan's dog is in Ms. Cook's room!"

Mr. Mills said, "Jan, you'll have to see that your dog gets back to your house. We can't have dogs in school. But don't be long. We're to sing songs, and that's lots of fun."

Jan took Rags back to the house and shut her in the kitchen. She rubbed her dog's neck. "I mopped this kitchen, so you be a good dog," she said.

Then Jan ran back to school to sing songs and have fun. But she was not back for long when the lunch bell rang.

When Jan got to the lunchroom, she looked for Dan and Pam. Then she went to sit with them. As she ripped her lunch sack, she said to Dan, "Rags got into Ms. Cook's room. I took her back to the house and shut her in the kitchen."

But Dan said, "Look! Rags is back!"

And Jan looked up to see Rags run into the lunchroom.

"She can't be back!" said Jan. "I shut her in the kitchen!"

But Rags was back. She ran up to a boy on a bench. Then she sat up and begged. The boy rubbed her on the neck and fed her bits of chicken from his lunch.

Jan had to get Rags. Rags was not happy when Jan took her back to the house. She shut Rags in the kitchen and locked it. Then she ran back to school. When she got back, the bell had rung.

Jan ran back into Mr. Mills's room. She had to tell Mr. Mills that Rags had run back into the school.

"Your dog will have to be locked in when you go to school," said Mr. Mills. "You didn't have much lunch, did you?"

"No," said Jan. "I will shut Rags in the kitchen and lock it. Then I will not have to miss lunch!"

"Well," said Mr. Mills, "I'll bet you'll have a good story to tell your mom and dad!"

Look It Up!

fixing

missing

passing

looking

sitting

humming

tapping

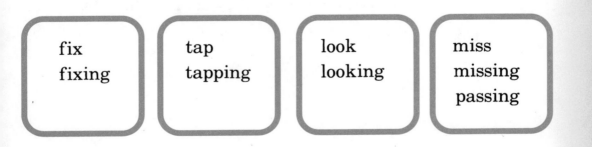

| fix
fixing | tap
tapping | look
looking | miss
missing
passing |

A Song on the Bells

Ms. King was sitting in her room at school. She was fixing her set of bells.

A little peg was missing from the set of bells. Ms. King fixed that with a bit of wood.

Ms. Cook was passing by Ms. King's room. Ms. King was humming a little song and tapping it on the bells.

Ms. Cook said, "I like that song. You got it from TV, didn't you?"

"Yes, I did," said Ms. King.

"Jim and Kim can sing that song well," Ms. Cook said.

"Then let's get them to sing it for my room and for yours," said Ms. King. "I can tap on the bells along with them."

"Good. I like that. I'll look for Kim and Jim," said Ms. Cook. But as she was looking for them, the bell rang. "I will look for them in the lunchroom," she said.

Jim and Kim were sitting in the lunchroom. Ms. Cook went up to them and said, "When you have had your lunch, will you go to my room? Ms. King and I wish to have you sing a song for us. Then you can sing it for my room and hers."

This is the song that Jim and Kim sang with Ms. King tapping along on the bells.

Sing along! Sing along,

As we go along.

Sitting on the bus

Is much fun for us.

Looking at things,

We go as on wings.

Humming a good song,

The trip is not long.

Sing along! Sing along!

On the Job

Sam was fixing his van. He was sitting in the cab of the van, looking at things and checking them.

Tam was passing by. She said, "Do you have room for me in the cab? I am good at fixing things."

Sam said, "Get in. I don't have much to do, but I can't get this lock fixed."

Tam got into the cab. She and Sam fixed the lock. They were happy as they did the job, humming a song.

Sam said, "You did that well, Tam. You are good at fixing things."

Lots of Pets

I have had a lot of pets. Let me tell you of them.

I had a dog I liked very much, but when he sat by me, did I itch! So I got a kitten. I __??__ my kitten very much, but when she __??__ by me, I did itch and itch! So then I got a horse. I liked my __??__ very much, but when he was by me I had a bad itch. I rubbed and rubbed.

Then I got a pet that was good for me. When I sat by it, I did not itch or __??__. My pet is a fish, and I like it very __??__.

mend

bend

send

lend

end

wind

Mrs.

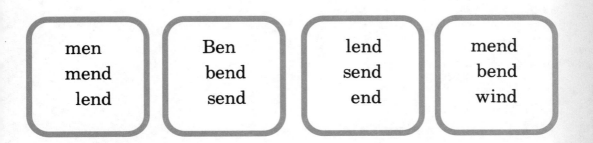

men	Ben	lend	mend
mend	bend	send	bend
lend	send	end	wind

The Bike Trip

Jim was sitting on a bench, looking at his bike. "I will have to mend it," he said to Tam. "I cannot lend my bike to Pam for her bike trip if I don't get it fixed."

Tam said, "You can get a little tin to fix that spot. You can bend it to fit."

"My bike will go like the wind when I get it fixed," said Jim.

"We can send Pam to that shop by her house for the tin," said Tam.

"Yes," said Jim, "she will get it for us." Jim went to Pam's house to see her.

Pam said, "Yes, I will get the tin. Will you lend me your bike for my trip when it's fixed?"

"Yes," said Jim.

Pam got the tin from the shop by her house and took it to Jim. "Can you bend it to fit the bad spot?" she said.

"I have to if I'm going to fix this bike," said Jim. "Yes, it will fit. I can mend that spot on the end of the fender. Then you can have the bike for your trip."

"Good," said Pam. "I like bike trips. I will have fun, but I will be good to your bike. I will get it back to you with no bad spots."

Pam took Jim's bike. It was a good bike, and she had lots of fun on it. When she got back, she took the bike to Jim.

"It was a good trip, Jim. I'm happy you let me have your bike," she said.

At Mrs. Benton's Shop

A big wind ran along the paths. It pitched cans on end. Jan had a chill. She was happy to go into Mrs. Benton's shop. The gas was on, and the shop was hot.

Jan had to get a mat for Rags's bed. She picked up a mat. Then Jan had to shop for the kids in her room at school. They were going to send a box to a sick boy. She looked at a book. It was ripped, so she set it back. "We can't mend things," she said.

Jan got Rags's mat, a good book, a bell, a cap, and jacks. The sixth thing she got was a bag of nuts.

As Jan went from the shop, the wind let up. She forgot the chill and ran to school.

Going on a Trip

Going on a trip?

Let's zip in a jet.

If we go by ship,

We can get wet.

Send us in a bus,

My house I don't miss.

A van is good for us.

It's fun to do this.

Going on a trip,

I like a bike and pack.

I'm like a funny ship,

If the wind is at my back.

band

sand

hand

fond

pond

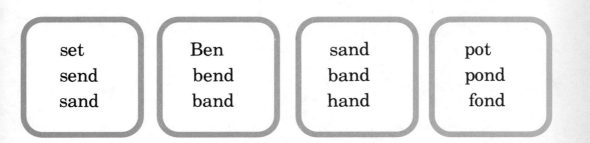

set	Ben	sand	pot
send	bend	band	pond
sand	band	hand	fond

Jobs for Ms. Long

Ms. Long had lots of little jobs to do at school. She was fond of her jobs. She hummed as she did them. She had to fix a big box for the school band. When she had fixed the box, she took it to Ms. Cook.

Ms. Cook said, "You did a good job. The band will be very happy. They can set lots of things in such a big box."

"Good," said Ms. Long. "I like to do things with my hands. I have to fix a sandbox for Mr. Little's room."

Ms. Long fixed the sandbox and took it to Mr. Little's room. She filled it with big bags of sand.

"This sandbox will be lots of fun," said Mr. Little. "You did a very good job."

"I like my job," said Ms. Long. "I have to get books from Ms. King and mend them. I have lots to do."

Then Ms. Long went to get the books. She took them back to her room. She was fond of her job, and she did it well.

Pam and a Fish

Pam was in her room at school. Ms. Cook said, "Pam, will you tell us a story?"

Pam liked to do that. "Yes," she said. "I can tell you a good fish story."

This is Pam's story.

I went fishing in a pond. I had a big hook on the end of my fishing rod. A big bug was on the hook.

A little fish was in the pond. It was a sunfish. The sunfish was fond of bugs. It looked at the bug on my hook, but it did not see that the bug was on the fishhook. So the fish got the bug. And the hook got the fish. Then I got the fish.

"Well," said Ms. Cook, "that's good, Pam. And I'll bet I can tell you the things the bug, the fish, and you said.

The bug said—

     Did you get me in your hand

     When you dug in the sand?

The fish said—

     Can you tell I am fond

     Of the bugs in my pond?

You said—

     Can you tell if you look

     That my rod has a hook?"

Then Ms. Cook said, "And can you tell me this—

     If you have a dish,

     Is it filled with fish?"

A Map

Hill Woods—

Bell Ranch—

Jet Pond—

Joy's Shop—

Fox School—

Will's House—

bent

lent

sent

dent

tent

pants

hunt

here

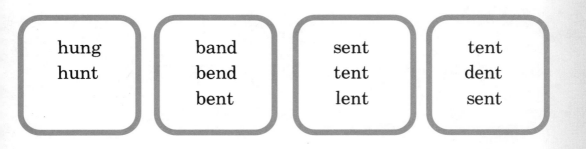

hung	band	sent	tent
hunt	bend	tent	dent
	bent	lent	sent

No Pens

"Dan! The school bus is passing by!" yelled Jan. "Get your lunch. Here is your jacket."

"But I have to look for my books and my pen," said Dan.

Dan went into the kitchen to hunt for his things. No books! No pens! Then he ran into his bedroom. "Here they are!" he yelled to Jan. "I've got my books, but I can't see my pen. Did I lend it to you?"

"No," said Jan. "Look in your tan pants."

"Here it is," said Dan, "but it's bent. It's no good. I'll have to hunt for a pen."

"You can have my red pen," said Jan. She sent him into her room for the pen.

"Look!" yelled Dan. "Rags got your pen. It has a dent in it!"

"That bad dog!" said Jan. "I'll have to set things up so Rags can't nip dents in them. I had a tan pen at school, but I lent it to Kim. Let's get going. A boy at school can lend you a pen."

"Let me look in here," said Dan. He hunted in a kit in the kitchen. A thick tablet, shells, and a pen were in it. "Here is a pen," said Dan, "and it's not bent."

"I forgot we had a pen in that kit," said Jan. "Let's go."

They had to run, but they got to school as the bell rang.

Let's Go Fishing

Dan and Jan had so much fun fishing at Grandma and Grandpa's. Jan went to her mom and said, "Can we go fishing? Can we fish in the pond by the woods?"

"That will be fun," said Mom. "Let's see if Dad and Dan will go with us."

Jan went to see if Dad and Dan wish to go.

"That will be lots of fun," said Dad. "We can pitch a tent by the pond. Then we can cook the fish we catch."

"I'll get things packed," said Dan. He got the tent, the fishing rods, and pots and pans.

When Dan had packed the things in the van, they hopped in. Into the woods they went till they got to a good spot by the pond.

Then Mom sent Jan to hunt for wood. Dan went to get the things from the van.

"Dad and I can pitch the tent here," said Mom. "Then we can go fishing."

So Mom and Dad got the tent set up. Jan hunted and hunted for wood. Then she went back to the spot by the pond. "I've looked and looked," she said, "but the wood is wet."

"Well, forget it," said Mom. "Let's go fishing. We can hunt for wood if we catch the fish."

They sat and sat by the pond with the fishing rods. But they didn't catch a fish. "No fish here," said Mom. "But it is a good spot to sit and look at the pond."

"Yes," said Jan, "we can have fun here."

"I have chicken wings and legs in the van,"

said Dad. "We can hunt for wood that's not wet. Then we can cook the chicken. We can have fun yet."

They went back to the tent. As Dad cooked chicken, Dan said, "We didn't catch fish. We didn't have good luck, but we did have fun!"

sink   bank

pink   sank

think   tank

ink   thank

bunk

junk

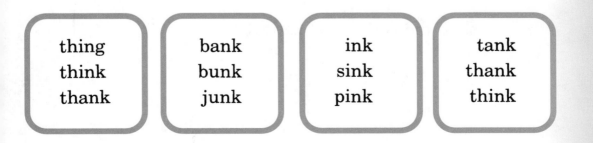

thing	bank	ink	tank
think	bunk	sink	thank
thank	junk	pink	think

At the Pet Shop

Mr. and Mrs. Benton had to cash a check. They were going to get bunk beds for Kim's room. Jim and Kim went with them when they went to the bank. They had to pass a pet shop to get to the bank. In the pet shop was a big tank of fish.

"I wish we had a tank of fish," said Kim.

"You can have a fish if you wish," said Mr. Benton.

"And a tank?" said Jim.

"If it's a little tank," said Mrs. Benton.

So they began to look for a little tank for a fish. They looked in the pet shop, but the shop didn't have a little fish tank.

So Mrs. Benton said, "I think I will go on to the bank. You can look for a little tank in that junk shop we passed."

The junk shop did have a little tank. So Jim got it and took it back to the pet shop.

"Can I have that big red fish?" said Jim to Mr. Benton.

"Yes," said Mr. Benton. "And you can have that pink fish if you like."

They had to dip a net into the big tank to catch the pink fish and the red fish. Then Mr. Benton picked up a little bag of sand and let the sand sink into the little tank. He let six pink shells sink onto the sand.

Kim looked at the shells as they sank. "I like that," she said.

When the fish were in the tank, they did not sink. They went by the shells to the end of the tank. Then they went to the top of the tank, and back to the shells.

"Thank you for the fish and the tank," said Jim and Kim.

When Mrs. Benton got back, she was rubbing her hand. "The pen at the bank got ink on my hand," she said. "Well, let's get the bunk beds."

Happy Fish

Jim said to Pam, "Let's go to my house. We have a pink fish and a red fish."

At the Bentons' house, the fish tank was in the kitchen by the sink. Pam said, "I think I like the pink fish. It looks as if it has ink spots on it."

"Do you think the fish are happy in the tank?" said Jim.

"If they get fed, they will be," said Kim. She took bits from a bag and filled the tank. The bits didn't sink. The fish went up to the top to get the bits.

"Look at the pink fish nip!" said Kim.

"The red fish is funny," said Pam. "I do think the fish are happy," Pam said to Jim.

The Boy in the Pond

I looked in the pond,
And I did see
A little boy.
He looked like me.

I sat.
He sat.
I looked at him,
And he looked back.

I got up,
And so did he,
That little boy.
He looked at me.

I think that I am very fond
Of that little boy in the pond.

last

fast

past

must

just

dust

fist

list

home

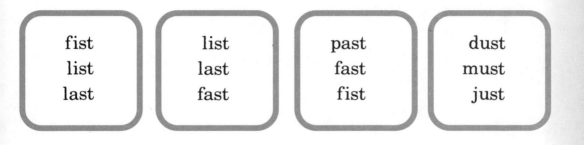

fist	list	past	dust
list	last	fast	must
last	fast	fist	just

Lists for Dinner

Mr. and Mrs. Bell were in the kitchen when Dan and Jan got home. Mr. Bell said, "Mr. Sands and Pam will be here for dinner. So we have lots to do. Here is a list."

Dad had a list for Dan and for Jan. Dan looked at his list. "I have to set the dinner things for us. But I will do that last. I must mop the kitchen and dust the bedrooms," said Dan.

Jan said, "I must run and get fish or chicken for dinner. When I get back, I must fix up the bathroom. I'll have to do the things on my list fast. I have things to do for school."

"I have just a little to do for school," said

Dan. "But I must pick up the mess in my room."

"Well, let's get going," said Jan. She ran past Dan.

Dan went into the kitchen. He got it mopped, and then he dusted the bedrooms. As he went back into the kitchen, Jan got home. She had a big sack of chicken in her fist.

"I like chicken better than fish," she said. "Dad cooks such good chicken, so I got lots. I'll go fix up the bathroom."

"Good," said Mrs. Bell. "Your dad can cook the chicken. Dan and I can set the dinner things. We will have to do things fast. Gus and Pam will be here in just a little bit."

Dad got going on the chicken. Dan and

Mom got the dinner things set up. Jan fixed up the bathroom.

"Well," said Dad, "the house looks good. The kitchen is mopped, and the bedrooms are dusted. The bathroom is fixed up. The chicken is cooked. But Gus and Pam aren't here."

Just then, the bell rang. Mom went to let Gus and Pam in, but it was a little boy with jam to sell. So Mom took the jam. When she went back into the kitchen, she said, "It wasn't Gus and Pam. It was a little boy selling jam for his school."

"They will be here in a little bit," said Dad. "It isn't six yet."

"Well, if they aren't here by six, I'll go to look for them," said Jan.

"No, you have things to do for school," said Dad. "I'll go."

So they just sat and sat. Then Dad said, "Well, it is past six. I must look for them."

Just then the bell rang. Dad went to let Gus and Pam in. Gus said, "I didn't forget dinner at your house. When I got home, Pam's hen wasn't in her pen. We hunted and hunted. When we got Little Red back, we went to the van. It had a bad lock, so I had to fix that. Then Pam fell and cut her leg. So much bad luck! Good luck for us will begin with dinner!"

Sunset

The sinking sun tints the sky red.

Sinking.

Sinking.

It sits on top of the hill,

but not for long.

Sinking.

Sinking.

Sinking.

At last, sunset.

best

rest

test

pest

west

nest

vest

chest

Grandfather

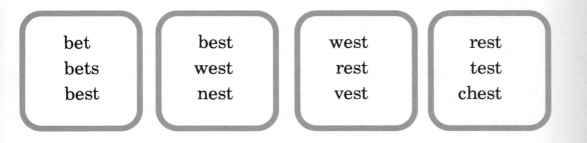

bet	best	west	rest
bets	west	rest	test
best	nest	vest	chest

A Hen and Her Nest

Kim and her mom were sitting in back of the house. Kim said, "Look, Mom! That is a robin's nest! Did you see that robin? Let's go look at the nest!"

"No," said Mom. "The robin will fuss. A robin can be as bad as a hen on a nest. Let me tell you a story of a hen and her nest."

When I was ten, we went west to Grandma and Grandpa's ranch. On the ranch were lots of chickens.

Of the chickens, I liked Grandma's red hen best. She didn't peck my hands, and she didn't yell much. The red hen was not a pest like the rest of the chickens.

When the red hen had eggs, she sat on her nest to hatch the eggs into chicks. She was on the nest when a fox ran into the chicken house.

From the house, I looked at the fox run in. "A fox just ran for the chicken's nest," I yelled to Grandfather. Grandfather shook his fist as we ran to the chicken house.

The red hen was hitting the fox with her wings. She pecked at the fox and yelled a lot. She didn't let the fox get her eggs.

When the fox looked at Grandfather and me, it ran into the woods. The red hen sat on her nest, happy to be rid of that pest.

The Shopping List

The Bentons had a long shopping list. "We have to pick up lots of things," Mrs. Benton said to Jim and Kim. "And we must look at bunk beds."

"Good," said Kim. "Let's go."

When they got to the shop with the bunk beds, Jim picked a bed he liked. Dad said, "You will have to test it, Jim."

So Jim went up the ladder to the top bed. The ladder had a bad rung. But Mr. Benton said, "I can fix that."

"I like this bed," said Jim.

"Good," said Mom. "We can get a chest to match it. This big chest looks best to me. Do you like it?"

"Yes, I do," said Jim.

"We will have to look for a bed and a chest for your room, Kim," said Mom.

"I like this bed," said Kim.

"Good," said Dad. "And this chest?"

"Yes," said Kim. "I think they will look best in my room."

The man in the shop said they had a van to get the beds and chests to the Bentons' house. "We must get the rest of the things on the list," said Dad. "I must get pants and a vest. Jim must have socks."

"Can I get a vest?" said Kim.

"Yes," said Mom, "that's on the list."

"Well," said Dad, "we have to get going. That's a long list."

The Bentons shopped and shopped. When they had the things on the list, they went home.

"Such a long list! Such a lot of things! Vests! Chests! Pants! Socks!" said Dad.

"I had fun," said Jim. "I like to go shopping."

mask

ask

desk

disk

lift

gift

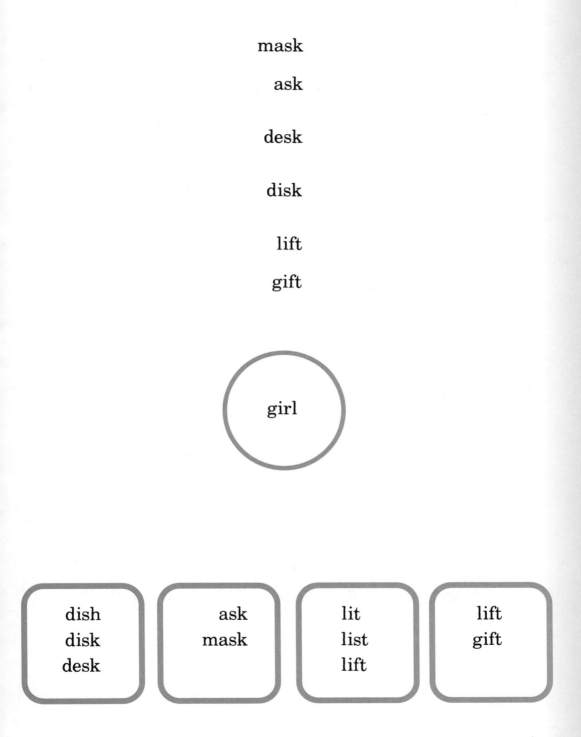

girl

dish	ask	lit	lift
disk	mask	list	gift
desk		lift	

A Gift for Pam

"Pam is such a good girl," said Gus Sands to Mr. Bell. "I have to think of a good gift for her, Tom."

"Did she ask for a gift?" asked Mr. Bell.

"No," said Mr. Sands, "but I will be happy to get her a gift. I was thinking of a desk. Do you think that's a good gift for my little girl?"

"I think so," said Mr. Bell. "I'll go with you to look at desks if you wish."

"That's good. Let's get going," said Mr. Sands.

Mr. Sands and Mr. Bell went to a shop and looked at lots and lots of desks. Then Mr. Sands said, "Tom, look at this desk. I think Pam will like it."

"Yes," said Mr. Bell. He looked at the desk. "It has a lid that lifts up and little wooden bins under the lid."

"Pam will not have to hunt for her things if she has this desk," said Mr. Sands. "It has bins for her pens and tablets."

"I think she will like it," said Mr. Bell.

"And it will match the bed and chest in her room," said Mr. Sands. "I will tell the shop to bill me. I think we can lift it onto my van."

"I have a big red ribbon for it," said Mr. Bell. "It's a good gift for a little girl."

The Math Test

Mr. Mills said, "I have a math test for you. It is not such a bad test. I think you will do well."

Kim's hand went up.

"Yes, Kim?" said Mr. Mills.

"Can we have the number disks?" Kim asked.

"Not when you have a test," said Mr. Mills. "I will do a set with you. Then just do your best."

So Mr. Mills did just a little of the test with the boys and girls. Then they did the rest.

Kim was fast with the test. Jan did not go as fast. When Jan took her test to Mr. Mills, she said, "I don't think I did well."

Mr. Mills said, "Well, let's see."

Mr. Mills took the test to his desk. Then he checked it. "Look, Jan," he said. "You did very well."

"Good," said Jan. "I'm happy then."

"You can go to lunch," said Mr. Mills. "We will fix up masks when you get back."

"Good," said Jan. "I like that better than math tests!"

Pat's Pets

	1	2	3	4	5	6	7	8	9	10
Dogs	■	■	■							
Cats	■	■								
Chickens	■	■	■	■	■	■	■	■	■	■
Ducks	■	■	■	■	■	■	■			
Pigs	■	■	■	■	■	■				
Horses	■	■	■	■	■					

As you can see, Pat has a lot of pets.

left

next

kept

help

held

day

play

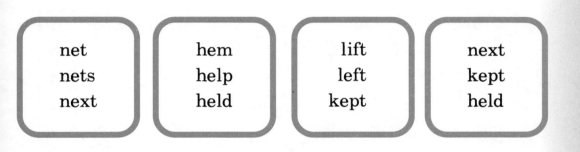

net	hem	lift	next
nets	help	left	kept
next	held	kept	held

Dan Can Help

Dan left school thinking of numbers. He liked math best in school. Numbers were like play to him. But when Ms. King asked Dan to tell a story, he began, and then forgot what to tell next. Or he didn't end the story. Ms. King said, "Thanks, Dan," but he wasn't happy with his story.

Dan went along a path next to the school. It was a hot day, but he kept his jacket on. He held onto his books and began to run. He ran until he kicked a rock. He lifted the rock, letting bugs run from the sun. Dan dusted the rock and set it in the path next to his books. He sat on the rock thinking.

"I can help a boy or girl in school who can't do numbers well. Helping with math is like play for me. If I do that, I may get a boy or girl to help me tell a story."

Dan lifted the rock to set it back. The bugs had run from the sun. Just then a robin began to sing.

"I may tell a story of a robin," Dan said looking up. "When I get home, I'll see if I can help Jim, Jan, or Kim. Then they can help me."

A Good Day

On the day of the math test, Pam's dad had a lot of shopping to do. He picked Pam up at school and took her to Dan and Jan's. "May Pam play at your house until I get back?" asked Mr. Sands.

"Yes," said Dan. "May she go on the bike path with us?"

"Well, if she is not by herself, it will be OK," Mr. Sands said.

When Mr. Sands had left, Jan said, "We will have to hunt for a bike for you, Pam."

"I think we can rent a bike at a spot by the path," said Dan.

Then Pam said, "Let's go!"

They went to the spot by the path and got Pam a bike. Then into the woods they went on the bike path.

They had so much fun. Then Pam said, "I have to get back. Dad is picking me up at six."

"We'll have to rush," said Jan.

They left Pam's bike at the spot by the path. When they got back, Mr. Sands was sitting in his van.

"I had a good day, Dad," said Pam.

"Good," said Mr. Sands. "Let's go. I have kept your dinner hot for you."

Good Things, Bad Things

It's a good thing I got up to go to school.

It's a bad thing my pants got ripped.

It's a good thing I can mend my pants.

It's a bad thing they will look a mess
   if I fix them.

It's a good thing I forgot—

  This is NOT a school day!

  I can go back to bed!

And isn't THAT a good thing?

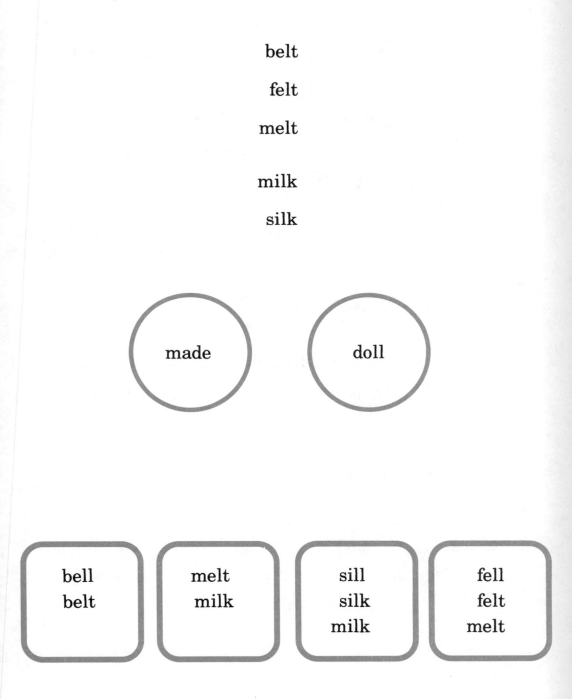

belt

felt

melt

milk

silk

made doll

bell	melt	sill	fell
belt	milk	silk	felt
		milk	melt

Masks for a Play

On a wet September day, Pam was playing in her room. She made masks for a play in her room at school. "Ms. Cook will like this mask," she said to herself. "It has silk on it to match my belt."

Just then, the bell rang. "Who is it?" said Pam.

"It's Tam!" yelled Tam.

"Good," said Pam as she ran to let Tam in. "You can look at the masks I made for the school play."

"Who helped you with them?" asked Tam.

"I made them myself," said Pam.

"You did a good job," said Tam. "I like that silk mask best."

"I like the felt mask," said Pam.

When Pam's room had the play at school, Mr. Sands went to see it. He took Tam with him. The boys and girls in the play had on the masks Pam had made.

Six of the boys and girls looked like ducks. Six looked like horses. The moms and dads who were at the play had lots of fun. It was a very funny play with Pam's very funny masks.

Chester's Story

When Pam got home on the day of the play, her puppy, Chester, ran to her. "I had a good day, Chester," said Pam. "But I'm so hot, I may melt. Let's play."

Mr. Sands said, "Chester has to be fed. Then he can play."

This is Chester's story—if you think a puppy can tell a story.

I am Chester, Pam's puppy. I am very fond of Pam. I think she likes me, but she likes to play that I am a doll. That gets me mad!

When Pam gets home from school I will run and get under her bed. I will not have that pink ribbon on me.

Pam has jackets and belts and silk ribbons

for her dolls. I don't like doll things on me. I don't like to rest on a doll's bed or have my milk from a doll's cup.

Pam must have felt sad when I hid from her. "I don't think Chester likes me," she said to her dad.

"Chester likes you, Pam," her dad said, "but not when you play that he is a doll. Set a dish of milk for him. I will get the ham I had left from dinner. Then I will help you look for Chester."

"They do not have to look for me," I said to myself. I like milk and ham. I like Pam and her dad. I just don't like to play that I am a doll!

The Wind and Me

The wind passed by today.

    It kicked

    and hopped

    and zipped

      along

and made little hills in the sand.

    And then

    it hummed

    a happy

      song

and took me by the hand.

jump

lump

bump

mumps

camp

lamp

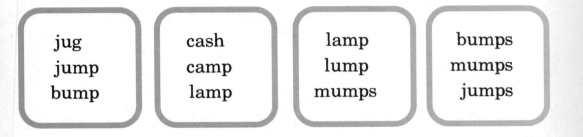

jug	cash	lamp	bumps
jump	camp	lump	mumps
bump	lamp	mumps	jumps

Bumps and Lumps

Dan felt sick. He felt a little bump on his leg. Then he got bumps on his neck and his chest. His mom said, "Well, it isn't mumps, but you can't go to school with such a rash."

"OK," said Dan, "but do I have to be in bed for the day?"

"No," said Mom. "You can sit in here and look at TV."

After a bit, Mrs. Bell went to look in on Dan. He had set up a little camp with a play tent. He and Rags were sitting in the tent.

"Sit next to the lamp," said Mom. "I have to look at your rash."

"OK," said Dan. "I don't think the bumps went away. And they itch and itch!"

"No," said Mom, "your rash did not go away. I wish you felt better. Have you rested?"

"Yes," said Dan.

"Well, I'll get your lunch," said Mom. "Maybe that will help."

After lunch, Dan said, "I think that helped."

"Good," said Mom. "I have to go."

When his mom left, Dan was sitting by the lamp looking at his math book.

Dan went back to school the next day. Ms. King asked him if he felt better.

"Much better," said Dan. "I had a rash, but it went away. It wasn't such a bad rash, but it itched. I do not have a lump or bump left."

"Well, I'm happy your mom and dad kept you at home. Did you have a good day?" asked Ms. King.

"Yes," said Dan, "but Rags kept jumping on me. She jumps a lot. She thinks I was at home just to play with her. I did not let her jump for long. I made her sit by me. Then I did my math."

"Good, then you will not have to catch up on the math you missed," said Ms. King.

"No," said Dan. "I did it at home."

Dan handed Ms. King the math that he had. She sat by her desk lamp and checked it.

"You did very well," she said to Dan as she handed his math back to him.

"Thanks," said Dan. "Did I do a better job than on the last math?"

"Much better," said Ms. King. "I'm very happy. If I can help you, just tell me."

When the bell rang, Dan jumped up to run home. He took his math to his mom and dad. "Look!" he said. "I think my lumps and bumps helped me with my math!"

TO THE TEACHER

The MERRILL READING PROGRAM consists of eight Readers developed on linguistic principles applicable to the teaching of reading. The rationale of the program and detailed teaching procedures are described in the Teacher's Edition of each Reader.

All words introduced in this Reader are listed on the following pages under the headings "Words in Pattern," "Sight Words," and "Applications of Patterning."

Words listed as "Words in Pattern" represent additional matrices in the first major set of spelling patterns. The new matrices in this Reader include all five vowel letters and the consonant-letter combinations *sh, ng, nd, nt, nk, st, sk, ft, xt, pt, lp, ld, lt, lk,* and *mp.* This Reader also introduces *sh* in initial position. Also presented are pattern words with the endings *-ed* and *-ing,* including forms in which the final consonant letter of the pattern word is doubled.

Words listed as "Sight Words" are high-frequency words introduced to provide normal sentence patterns in the stories.

Words listed as "Applications of Patterning" include new words based on patterns and sight words previously introduced, combinations of words (compound words), additional tense forms, plurals, possessives, and contractions.

WORD LISTS FOR TEACHER REFERENCE

Pages	Words in Pattern	Sight Words	Pages	Words in Pattern	Sight Words
Unit 1 5-12	shop shot ship shut shed shell shack	from house	Unit 6 37-42	ripped mopped begged rubbed	when
Unit 2 13-18	fish wish dish rash hash mash cash	don't Mr. trip	Unit 7 43-48	fixing missing passing looking sitting humming tapping	
Unit 3 19-24	rang hang sang bang long song	boy who they	Unit 8 49-54	mend bend send lend end wind	Mrs.
Unit 4 25-30	ring sing king wing thing	like bike were	Unit 9 55-60	band sand hand fond pond	
Unit 5 31-36	hung rung	room school Ms.	Unit 10 61-66	bent lent sent dent tent pants hunt	here

Pages	Words in Pattern	Sight Words
Unit 11 67-72	sink pink think ink bunk junk bank sank tank thank	
Unit 12 73-78	last fast past must just dust fist list	home
Unit 13 79-84	best rest test pest west nest vest chest	Grandfather

Pages	Words in Pattern	Sight Words
Unit 14 85-90	mask ask desk disk lift gift	girl
Unit 15 91-96	left next kept help held	day play
Unit 16 97-102	belt felt melt milk silk	made doll
Unit 17 103-107	jump lump bump mumps camp lamp	

Applications of Patterning
(The underlined numbers are page numbers.)

Unit 1
5-12

cookbooks
hooks
mug
shells
ships
tots
vans
woodshed

Unit 2
13-18

forget
Gus's
kissed
mashed
packed
yams
yours

Unit 3
19-24

Benton
ditch
shacks
sheds
songs

Unit 4
25-30

along
bikes
chicken
cooks
I'm
kings
rings
things
wings

Unit 5
31-36

aren't
begin
Cook's
didn't
he's
jacket
jackets
Mills
Mills's
tablet

Unit 6
37-42

bathroom
bedrooms
dog's
I'll
kitchen
lunchroom
we're
you'll

Unit 7
43-48

cab
checking
hers
kitten
liked

Unit 8
49-54

Benton's
fender
forgot
funny
gas
going
Rags's
sixth
trips

Unit 9
55-60

fishhook
fishing
hands
hook
hummed
jobs
Joy's
Little's
rod
sandbox
sunfish
Will's

Unit 10
61-66

bedroom
dents
hopped
hunted
I've
rods
till

Unit 11
67-72

began
Bentons'
net
onto
passed
rubbing

Unit 12
73-78

better
dinner
dusted
isn't
lists
or
Sands
sell
selling
sinking
sunset
tints
wasn't

Applications of Patterning

(The underlined numbers are page numbers.)

Unit 13 79-84	Unit 14 85-90	Unit 15 91-96	Unit 16 97-102	Unit 17 103-107
Bentons	asked	helping	belts	after
chests	bins	hem	Chester	away
chicken's	boys	herself	Chester's	bumps
chickens	checked	letting	dads	handed
eggs	desks	lifted	doll's	itched
hatch	disks	may	dolls	jumped
hitting	girls	nets	helped	jumping
ladder	lit	numbers	jackets	jumps
robin	lifts	OK	likes	lumps
robin's	masks	picking	moms	maybe
shook	number	rent	myself	rested
shopped	ribbon	rush	playing	
shopping	tablets	thanks	puppy	
vests	tests	until	ribbons	
yell	thinking	we'll	September	
	under		today	
	wooden		zipped	